日蓮正宗について

日蓮正宗は、建長5（1253）年4月28日に、日蓮大聖人が「南無妙法蓮華経」の宗旨を建立されたことに始まります。

日蓮大聖人は、釈尊の滅後2000年が経過し、尊仏法の功力がなくなった末法時代に、法華経の証通り、民衆を救済する仏として出現されました。

日蓮大聖人は、法華経の極理を御本尊（漫荼羅）として顕され、その御本尊に向かって「南無妙法蓮華経」の題目を唱えることにより、いかなる人も成仏という真の幸福境界に至ることができると説かれました。

そして、弘安2（1279）年10月12日、信仰の根本である本門戒壇の大御本尊を建立されました。

その後、白蓮阿闍梨日興上人を第2祖と定めて仏法の一切を付嘱し、同5年10月13日、61歳をもって入滅されました。

以来700有余年、日蓮大聖人の仏法は、日興上人より第3祖日目上人へ、日目上人より第4世日道上人と、一器の水を一器に瀉ぐが如く相承され、御当代・68世日如上人まで、正しく伝えられています。

現在、日蓮正宗を信仰する人々の輪は、世界50カ国以上に広がっており、総本山大石寺のほか、国内に700以上、海外にも30以上ある寺院・布教所等において、多くの人々が信仰の喜びを体験しています。

What is Nichiren Shoshu?

Nichiren Shoshu began from Nichiren Daishonin's declaration of the Establishment of True Buddhism of Nam-Myoho-Renge-Kyo on the twenty-eighth day of the fourth month of the fifth year of Kenchō (1253).

Two thousand years after the passing of Shakyamuni Buddha, the benefit and power of Shakyamuni Buddha's Buddhism were lost in the Latter Day of the Law. As predicted in the Lotus Sutra, Nichiren Daishonin made his advent in this age as the True Buddha who would save the people.

Nichiren Daishonin manifested the ultimate principle of the Lotus Sutra as the Gohonzon (*Mandala*). He further preached that everyone can truly attain peace and happiness in their life, which is also referred to as the attainment of Buddhahood through the chanting of the Daimoku, Nam-Myoho-Renge-Kyo, to the Gohonzon.

On the twelveth day of the tenth month of the second year of Kō'an (1279), Nichiren Daishonin inscribed the Dai-Gohonzon of the High Sanctuary of the Essential Teaching, which is the foundation of faith and practice in Nichiren Shoshu Buddhism.

After selecting Byakuren Ajari Nikko Shonin as the Second High Priest and transferring the entirety of his teachings to him, Nichiren Daishonin passed away on the thirteenth day of the tenth month of the fifth year of Kō'an (1282) at the age of 61.

Just as the water in a vessel is poured into another, the Heritage of the Law of Nichiren Daishonin's Buddhism was inherited from Nikko Shonin to Third High Priest Nichimoku Shonin, and from Nichimoku Shonin to Fourth High Priest Nichido Shonin. Furthermore, it has been correctly transferred from the successive High Priests to Sixty-eighth High Priest Nichinyo Shonin in the present age for over 700 years after the passing of Nichiren Daishonin.

Today, the believers of Nichiren Shoshu are in more than 50 countries in the world. In addition to the Head Temple Taisekiji, there are more than 700 Nichiren Shoshu local temples and propagation centers in Japan, with over 30 outside of Japan. Now, many people are practicing Nichiren Shoshu Buddhism and are experiencing the delights of faith all over the world.

日蓮正宗総本山大石寺　三　門
Nichiren Shoshu Head Temple Taisekiji Sammon Gate

総本山大石寺

　総本山大石寺は、正応3年（1290）10月、宗祖日蓮大聖人から付嘱を承けられた第2祖日興上人によって開創されました。

　大石寺には、宗旨の根本である本門戒壇の大御本尊が厳護されており、日蓮大聖人以来の血脈を所持される御法主上人がおられます。したがって、大石寺は日蓮大聖人の仏法の一切と御精神が脈々と息づいている霊地なのです。

　日蓮大聖人が「須弥山に近づく鳥は金色となる」（本尊供養御書）と仰せのように、大石寺に参詣し本門戒壇の大御本尊にお目通りすることによって、私達は自らの罪障を消滅し、諸々の願いを成就して、成仏の大道を歩むことができるのです。

　日蓮正宗総本山大石寺こそ唯一、宗祖日蓮大聖人の教えを正しく今日に伝え、世界の民衆を真に救済する根本道場なのです。

Head Temple Taisekiji

　Head Temple Taisekiji was established in the tenth month of the third year of Shō'ō (1290) by Second High Priest Nikko Shonin, who was transferred the Heritage of the Law from the founder, Nichiren Daishonin.

　Taisekiji is where the Dai-Gohonzon of the High Sanctuary of the Essential Teaching, the fundamental of Nichiren Shoshu Buddhism, is securely stored and the successive High Priest, who have inherited the Lifeblood Heritage of the Law from Nichiren Daishonin, resides. Therefore, Head Temple Taisekiji is the sacred place where the entirety of Nichiren Daishonin's Buddhism and his spirit ceaselessly exist.

　Nichiren Daishonin states in *On Offerring to the Gohonzon* (Honzon kuyo gosho), "A bird that approaches Mount Sumeru will shine with a golden hue." As he expounds, we can eradicate our negative karma, have our prayers answered, and advance toward the attainment of Buddhahood by making tozan pilgrimage to Head Temple Taisekiji and having an audience with the Dai-Gohonzon of the High Sanctuary of the Essential Teaching.

　Head Temple Taisekiji of Nichiren Shoshu is the one and only fundamental place for the faith and practice of True Buddhism, where the teaching of the founder Nichiren Daishonin is correctly inherited up until today, to truly save the people in the world.

登山参詣
―本門戒壇の大御本尊を求めて―
Tozan Pilgrimage
― Yearning for the Dai-Gohonzon of the High Sanctuary of the Essential Teaching ―

本門戒壇の大御本尊が御安置されている奉安堂前に集結した海外信徒

The overseas believers assembled in front of the Hōandō, where the Dai-Gohonzon of the High Sanctuary of the Essential Teaching resides.

各国の信徒が伝える信仰の喜び
~国別写真集~

The Joy of Faith Delivered by Overseas Believers
~ Photo Collection of Overseas Countries ~

日蓮正宗の信徒は、日々、増加し、世界には５０カ国以上にわたり信仰の喜びを実感しております。

The number of Nichiren Shoshu believers is increasing day by day. Now, in more than 50 countries, they are practicing Nichiren Daishonin's Buddhism and experiencing great joy of this faith.

大韓民国
Korea

金海国際空港 International Airport 2時間20分

台湾桃園国際空港 Taiwan Taoyuan International Airport 3時間50分

空港（日本国内）までの所要時間 Traveling Time to the Airports (in Japan)

台　湾
Taiwan

アジア・オセアニア　Asia and Oceania

空港(日本国内)までの所要時間
Traveling Time to the Airports (in Japan)

香港国際空港
Hong Kong International Airport 5h 05m

マニラ ニノイ・アキノ国際空港
Ninoy Aquino International Airport 4h 50m

アジア・オセアニア Asia and Oceania

 香港 Hong Kong

 フィリピン Philippines

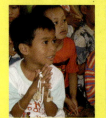

バンコク　スワナブーム国際空港　7時間00分
Suvarnabhumi International Airport

クアラルンプール国際空港　7時間35分
Kuala Lumpur International Airport

空港（日本国内）までの所要時間
Traveling Time to the Airports (in Japan)

タ　イ
Thailand

マレーシア
Malaysia

アジア・オセアニア　Asia and Oceania

11

空港（日本国内）までの所要時間　シンガポール・チャンギ国際空港　7時間25分　　ジャカルタ・スカルノハッタ国際空港　8時間00分
Traveling Time to the Airports (in Japan)　Singapore changi International Airport　　　　Jakarta International Soekarno-Hatta Airport

アジア・オセアニア　Asia and Oceania

シンガポール / Singapore

インドネシア / Indonesia

12

| シドニー国際空港 Sydney Airport 9h 30m | オークランド国際空港 Auckland International Airport 10h 50m | 空港(日本国内)までの所要時間 Traveling Time to the Airports (in Japan) |

 オーストラリア Australia

 ニュージーランド New Zealand

アジア・オセアニア Asia and Oceania

13

| 空港（日本国内）までの所要時間 Traveling Time to the Airports (in Japan) | デリー インディラ・ガンディー国際空港 Indira Gandhi International Airport | 9時間00分 | ムンバイ チャトラパティ・シヴァジー国際空港 Chhatrapati Shivaji International Airport | 9時間45分 |

アジア・オセアニア Asia and Oceania

インド
India

| コロンボ　バンダラナイケ国際空港 9時間30分 Bandaranaike International Airport | オスロ空港 12時間45分 Oslo Airport | ストックホルム・アーランダ国際空港 12時間50分 Stockholm-Arlanda International Airport | 空港(日本国内)までの所要時間 Traveling Time to the Airports (in Japan) |

スリランカ
Sri Lanka

ノルウェー
Norway

スウェーデン
Sweden

ヨーロッパ Europe

15

空港(日本国内)までの所要時間
Traveling Time to the Airports (in Japan)

コペンハーゲン国際空港 Copenhagen Airport　11時間35分 / 11h 35m

ロンドン・ヒースロー空港 London heathrow Airport　13時間00分 / 13h 00m

ヨーロッパ　Europe

デンマーク
Denmark

イギリス
U.K.

16

| ダブリン空港
Dublin Airport | 16時間10分 | フランクフルト国際空港
Frankfurt Intl.Airport | 11時間45分 | スキポール空港
Schiphol Airport | 12時間05分 | 空港（日本国内）までの所要時間
Traveling Time to the Airports (in Japan) |

アイルランド
Ireland

ドイツ
Germany

オランダ
Netherlands

ヨーロッパ　Europe

17

ヨーロッパ Europe

パリ　シャルル・ド・ゴール国際空港　Charles de Gaulle International Airport　12h 40m

フランス
France

ウィーン国際空港　Vienna International Airport　12h 05m

オーストリア
Austria

| チューリッヒ空港 Zurich Airport | 12時間25分 | ローマ フィウミチーノ空港 Fiumicino Airport | 12時間40分 | ベオグラード・ニコラ・テスラ空港 Belgrade Nikola Tesla Airport | 13時間20分 | 空港(日本国内)までの所要時間 Traveling Time to the Airports (in Japan) |

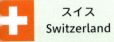
スイス
Switzerland

イタリア
Italy

セルビア
Serbia

ヨーロッパ　Europe

空港(日本国内)までの所要時間
Traveling Time to the Airports (in Japan)

マドリード・バラハス国際空港 14時間15分
Madrid-Barajas Airport 14h 15m

リスボン・ポルテラ空港 17時間20分
Lisbon Portela Airport 17h 20m

ヨーロッパ　Europe

スペイン
Spain

ポルトガル
Portugal

20

アクラ コトカ国際空港 Kotoka International Airport 19h05m　　　ロメ国際空港 Lome-Tokoin International Airport 18h45m　空港（日本国内）までの所要時間 Traveling Time to the Airports (in Japan)

ガーナ Ghana

トーゴ Togo

アフリカ Africa

21

空港(日本国内)までの所要時間　アビジャン　フェリックス・ウフェ・ボワニ国際空港　17時間30分　コトヌー　カジェフォウン空港　20時間00分　ブラザヴィル　マヤマヤ空港　20時間30分
Traveling Time to the Airports (in Japan)　Felix Houphouet Boigny International Airport　Cadjehoun Airport　Maya-Maya Airport

アフリカ　Africa

コートジボアール
Cote d'Ivoire

ベナン
Benin

コンゴ共和国
Republic of Congo

22

アブジャ ンナムディ・アジキウェ国際空港 **18**h**25**m
Nnamdi Azikiwe International Airport

ケープタウン国際空港 **19**h**20**m
Cape Town International Airport

空港(日本国内)までの所要時間
Traveling Time to the Airports (in Japan)

ナイジェリア
Nigeria

南アフリカ
South Africa

アフリカ Africa

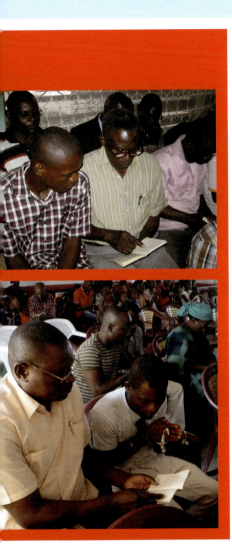

ANNUAL GENERAL MEETING OF MEMBERS IN NIGERIA HELD AT ENUGU STATE IN NIGERIA

23

北アメリカ / North America

 カナダ
Canada

 アメリカ
U.S.A.

ニューヨーク　ジョン・F・ケネディ国際空港　13h 05m
John F. Kennedy International Airport

空港（日本国内）までの所要時間
Traveling Time to the Airports (in Japan)

北アメリカ　North America

25

空港(日本国内)までの所要時間
Traveling Time to the Airports (in Japan)

メキシコ・シティ国際空港 13時間30分
Mexico City International Airport 13h 30m

トリニダード ピアルコ国際空港 トバゴ クラウン・ポイント空港 15時間
Piarco International Airport Crown Point Airport 15h

北アメリカ North America

メキシコ
Mexico

トリニダード・トバゴ
Trinidad and Tobago

パナシティー　トキュメン国際空港　17h 50m
Tocumen International Airport

サンホセ　ファン・サンタ・マリア国際空港　18h 00m
Juan Santamaria International Airport

空港〈日本国内〉までの所要時間
Traveling Time to the Airports (in Japan)

パナマ
Panama

コスタリカ
COSTA RICA

北アメリカ　North America

27

ブラジル
Brazil

リマ　ホルヘ・チャベス国際空港 Jorge Chávez International Airport 20h 20m
サンティアゴ　アルトゥーロ・メリノ・ベニテス国際空港 Comodoro Arturo Merino Benitez International Airport 26h 30m
空港（日本国内）までの所要時間 Traveling Time to the Airports (in Japan)

ペルー Peru

チリ Chile

南アメリカ South America

南アメリカ South America

アルゼンチン Argentina

ウルグアイ Uruguay

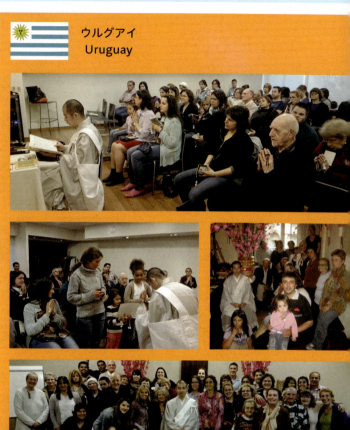

* ここに掲載した「空港（日本国内）までの所要時間」は参考値であり、実際の経路や季節等により、時間の変動があります。また、登山の際には、飛行時間以外に、自宅から現地空港、日本国内空港から総本山までの移動時間があります。

* "Traveling Time to the Airports (in Japan)" refers to the actual flight time between the airports in Japan and international airports in respective countries. However there may be variations in this time depending on the specific route taken, season, et al. When pilgrimaging to the Head Temple, in addition to flight time, there are further travel times to be considered, such as from the member's home to their local airport, and from the airports in Japan to the Head temple.

～国別写真集～

信仰の喜びが世界に！
―正しい教えが全民衆を救う―

平成27年8月26日　発行

監　修　　日蓮正宗宗務院海外部
編集・発行　株式会社　大日蓮出版
　　　　　418-0116
　　　　　静岡県富士宮市上条546番地の1

Ⓒ 大日蓮出版　2015

※本書を無断で転載・複製することを禁じます。

～ Photo Collection of Overseas Countries ～

The Joy of Faith Spread into the World
— The True Teaching Saves All Living Beings —

Published on August 26, 2015

Editorial Supervision by the Overseas Department, Nichiren Shoshu Head Office

Edited and Published by Dainichiren Publishing Co., Ltd.
546-1 Kamijo, Fujinomiya, Shizuoka, 418-0116, Japan

Ⓒ Dainichiren Publishing Co., Ltd. 2015

All rights reserved

上記の国々にも日蓮正宗の信徒が多数おります。
There are also Nichiren Shoshu believers in the above countries.

ISBN978-4-905522-43-0
C0415 ¥93 E

定価 (本体93円+税)

大日蓮出版

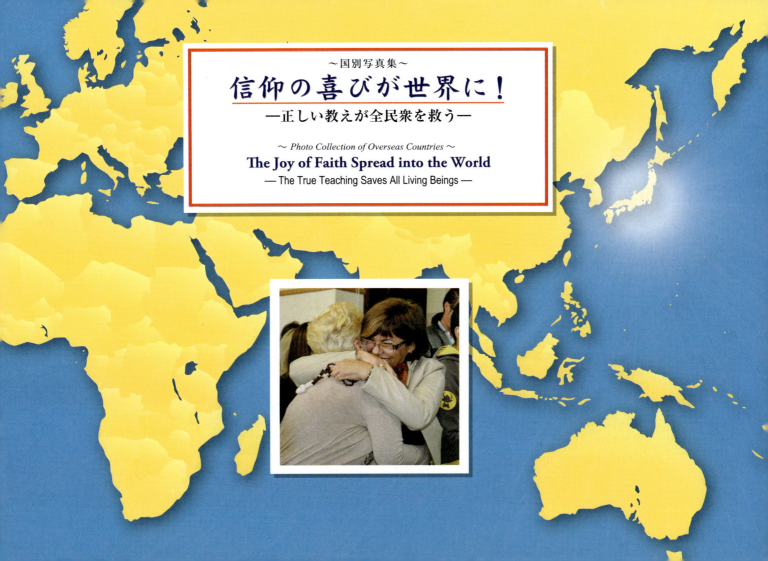

目次

日蓮正宗について / 3
総本山大石寺 / 4
登山参詣
― 本門戒壇の大御本尊を求めて ― / 5
世界に広がる日蓮正宗 / 6
各国の信徒が伝える信仰の喜び
～国別写真集～ / 8

アジア・オセアニア / 8
大韓民国 / 8　台湾 / 9　香港 / 10　フィリピン / 10　タイ / 11
マレーシア / 11　シンガポール / 12　インドネシア / 12
オーストラリア / 13　ニュージーランド / 13　インド / 14　スリランカ / 15

ヨーロッパ / 15
ノルウェー / 15　スウェーデン / 15　デンマーク / 16　イギリス / 16
アイルランド / 17　ドイツ / 17　オランダ / 17　フランス / 18　オーストリア / 18
スイス / 19　イタリア / 19　セルビア / 19　スペイン / 20　ポルトガル / 20

アフリカ / 21
ガーナ / 21　トーゴ / 21　コートジボアール / 22　ベナン / 22
コンゴ共和国 / 22　ナイジェリア / 23　南アフリカ / 23

北アメリカ / 24
カナダ / 24　アメリカ / 25　メキシコ / 26　トリニダード・トバゴ / 26
パナマ / 27　コスタリカ / 27

南アメリカ / 28
ブラジル / 28　ペルー / 29　チリ / 29　アルゼンチン / 30　ウルグアイ / 30

Contents

What is Nichiren Shoshu? / 3
Head Temple Taisekiji / 4
Tozan Pilgrimage
— Yearning for the Dai-Gohonzon of the High Sanctuary of the Essential Teaching — / 5
World Wide Propagation of Nichiren Shoshu Buddhism / 6
The Joy of Faith Delivered by Overseas Believers
～ Photo Collection of Overseas Countries ～ / 8

Asia and Oceania / 8
Korea / 8　Taiwan / 9　Hong Kong / 10　Philippines / 10　Thailand / 11
Malaysia / 11　Singapore / 12　Indonesia / 12
Australia / 13　New Zealand / 13　India / 14　Sri Lanka / 15

Europe / 15
Norway / 15　Sweden / 15　Denmark / 16　U.K. / 16
Ireland / 17　Germany / 17　Netherlands / 17　France / 18　Austria / 18
Switzerland / 19　Italy / 19　Serbia / 19　Spain / 20　Portugal / 20

Africa / 21
Ghana / 21　Togo / 21　Cote d'Ivoire / 22　Benin / 22
Republic of Congo / 23　Nigeria / 23　South Africa / 23

North America / 24
Canada / 24　U.S.A. / 25　Mexico / 26　Trinidad and Tobago / 26
Panama / 27　Costa Rica / 27

South America / 28
Brazil / 28　Peru / 29　Chile / 29　Argentina / 30　Uruguay / 30